The
RiDiCULOUSLY
EASY GUIDE™ to

Getting Along Better with Your Woman

PAULA SATOW

A Ridiculously Easy Guide™ Book

Published by Satow Strategies LLC

8902 E. Via Linda #110 - 118, Scottsdale, AZ 85258

info@satowstrategies.com

www.RidiculouslyEasyGuide.com.

ISBN: 978-0-9836332-0-4

The information in this book is designed to be a fun, easy way to
foster understanding and is not meant to replace professional
relationship programs or counseling.

Dedication

To my husband, David,
and my children, Rachel and Evan.
Thank you for your love and support.
My life is more wonderful because of you.

Acknowledgements

I wish to thank Vickie Mullins of Mullins Creative (www.MullinsCreative.com) – Independent Publishing Division – for her outstanding support of this book – from design to publication support. Her encouragement and expertise were vital components of the project's success.

I would also like to thank Jill Schildhouse (www.linkedin.com/in/jillschildhouse) for her insightful proofreading work.

Introduction

If you're thumbing through this book, or if your woman handed it to you with a note saying, "Read this or else!," then you're probably in need of a *Ridiculously Easy* way to improve your relationship. You've come to the right place.

My first draft of this book was a kind of love note for my husband, David, to help him understand what makes me tick (and what ticks me off) when it comes to our communications. At times, there seemed to be a disconnect between us and I wanted to get to the bottom of it. The fix was so obvious to me, but for him … not so much. Was that because, as a professional business communicator, I spend my days transforming complex messages into simple, digestible sound bites? Or because I've experienced a few "key learnings" from my previous relationships? Or was it simply that, while I am no expert on human psychology, I *am* an expert on ME and what makes ME happy.

No matter what the reason, one day, while in a midst of a particularly frustrating conversation (Perhaps that's why they call it "*con*-versation") with David, I suggested, "Look, it's ridiculously easy. All it takes is 1-2-3…" and I proceeded to explain in three easy steps what would make the conversation more satisfying to me. All of a sudden, he looked like a light bulb went off in his head and he responded, "Well, when you put it that way, it makes a lot of sense." Breakthrough! Write it down! I felt inspired and spent the next several hours capturing what I had told him into a little "guidebook" of sorts. Over the next few weeks, he patiently tested out my suggestions and, amazingly, it helped us begin to break through and improve our communications. When I saw how well the process worked for us, I felt inspired, yet again, to expand the book's reach from one hubby — to hubbies everywhere, not to mention significant others, boyfriends, life partners. And *The Ridiculously Easy Guide*™ was born.

I hope *The Ridiculously Easy Guide to Getting Along Better with Your Woman* not only helps you see the light in your communications, but also helps you see the **love**light in her eyes again! While there are no guarantees, I am confident that by following these **three** easy steps, the **two** of you can again feel like **one** — and your relationship can blastoff to new heights.

~ Paula Satow
Ridiculously Easy publisher and author

Publisher's Note
My vision is that this is the first of many *Ridiculously Easy Guide*™ books on different topics and by different authors. What will set *Ridiculously Easy*

Guide™ books apart is that they will be designed to make an important and complex subject ***Ridiculously Easy*** to understand and to learn in three easy steps. Please contact us at info@RidiculouslyEasyGuide.com if you would like to learn more about the series.

MICHAEL
(Hopefully)

Listen ... you know – I was a better
man with you ... as a woman ... with
you ... than I ever was as a man ...
with a woman ... I just have to
learn to do it without the dress.

~ Larry Gilbert,
Screenplay for the movie,
Tootsie

Quick Guide
... to Getting Along Better with Your Woman

Finally! Getting along better with your woman is as easy as 1–2–3! When your goal is to connect with her, suddenly you're talking her language. Apply these three easy steps to make it *Ridiculously Easy* to get along better with your woman. Read on to learn how.

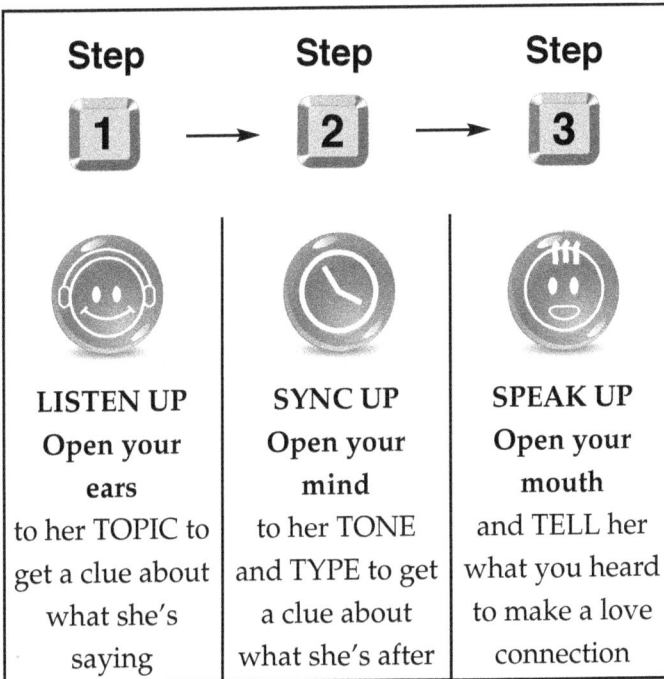

Step 1	Step 2	Step 3
LISTEN UP	**SYNC UP**	**SPEAK UP**
Open your ears	**Open your mind**	**Open your mouth**
to her TOPIC to get a clue about what she's saying	to her TONE and TYPE to get a clue about what she's after	and TELL her what you heard to make a love connection

Step 1

Listen Up

In Step 1, your job is to Listen Up.

Sounds *Ridiculously Easy*, right? Then why does she often say, "You never listen to me!"?

Perhaps because you're listening, but not in the way she needs. Author and interpersonal communications expert, Deborah Tannen, Ph.D., said, "For most women, the language of conversation is primarily a language of rapport." Tannen refers to this as "rapport-talk." [1] When your woman speaks, it's undoubtedly music to your ears, but the tune you may be hearing in your head is ...

"Here I come to save the day … that means that **AnswerMan** is on the way!"

That's because, according to Tannen, while women are all about rapport-talk, men are all about "report-talk" where they strive to "preserve independence" and "maintain status."[2] Guess what? The role of AnswerMan won't get you very far in the boudoir! To your credit, you want to be there for her. But according to author and relationship guru, John Gray (of *Men are from Mars, Women are from Venus* fame), a man's natural tendency is to offer a solution to his woman, even when there's not necessarily a problem. Gray explains in *Mars and Venus Together Forever*, "When a man loves a woman, his primary goal is to make her happy … . To him, her unhappiness means he is a failure."[3] Suddenly, a man's motivation to try to fix things that may not even broken becomes more clear. As it turns out, what a woman wants when she is reaching out in conversation may not be the AnswerMan or Mr. Fix-It but a **Listening Post** instead.

I know. It doesn't sound very sexy but, take it from me, it is to her! She longs for someone she loves and respects to be a sounding board for her — a safe place to reflect on the day, to bounce off ideas and to share observations. And since you are her first choice, you can feel flattered!

So, don't jump into solution space in Step 1. When you do, you stop listening and start thinking up fixes for problems that may not even exist. What seems like a simple conversation can turn on a dime into a *Ridiculously Complex* misunderstanding. You may feel frustrated because she doesn't give you credit for trying to help her ... *again*. And she may feel frustrated because you're talking about what you think instead of listening to what she thinks ... *again*.

Sound familiar?

Actively focus on the TOPIC at hand and what your woman is actually saying about it. Even if you're momentarily distracted or not particularly interested in what she's saying (Unthinkable, right?), you are interested in her and that's what matters. This is known as "active listening," which, according to Wikipedia, "is a structured way of listening and responding to others, focusing attention on the speaker. Suspending one's own frame of reference, suspending judgment and avoiding other internal mental activities are important to fully attend to the speaker."[4] So put down the remote, stop checking your smart phone and give it that old college try, OK? By the way, think back to the early beginnings of your relationship. Ask yourself, "Did I listen more? Did she feel better talking with me in those days than she does now?" If the answer is, "Yes," then you know you can do better. It's just a matter of brushing up on your skills!

When you actively focus on what your woman is saying, an interesting thing happens. Your capacity for understanding her skyrockets, bringing you a step closer toward your goal of getting along better. To you, communicating might be all about solving problems quickly, but to her, communicating literally translates as commune-icating … communing, conversing, connecting. Yes, the topic at hand is important to her — the kids, the car, her job, or what's for dinner — but feeling connected to you is even more important to her.

I know … WIIFM, right? What's In It For Me? The answer to that question is also *Ridiculously Easy*. When you hit the mark and the two of you connect, you'll both benefit. When connecting trumps winning, you're on the way to winning her heart. Things will click, you'll feel more relaxed and so will your shared conversational style. The two of you will finally be able to spend more relationship time actually "relating" instead of fussing over details or worrying about who is right or wrong. Instead of one of you winning and the other losing, all of a sudden you both win! Oh, and as an added bonus, when she feels more fulfilled in the Communications Department, fulfillment in some other departments may get easier too. Catch my drift?

So close your mouth, open your ears, and open your mind to the possibilities that lie ahead when you switch into LISTENING mode.

I hope you paid close attention (and listened) to Step 1 because there will be a test! It's called Step 2 ...

Quick Tip

➤ The Doghouse

Unless you're a dog, your ears don't wiggle when you LISTEN UP. But your body language lets her know you're listening. Try a little eye contact, adjusting your stance and/or softening your expression. It just may keep you out of the doghouse!!

Step 2

Sync Up

In Step 2, your job is to SYNC UP and get on the same wavelength.

Sound *Ridiculously Easy*?

It is easy ... when you go beyond the TOPIC you listened to in Step 1 and think about the TONE and TYPE of her communications in Step 2. In a sense, to SYNC UP is really to THINK UP about what you heard. In other words, apply the old adage and, "Think before you speak."

TONE is the feeling she is projecting when she speaks.

Her tone of voice and the way she is holding herself signal a lot about where she is coming from when she is talking to you. Why do you think they call it "body language"? Does she seem relaxed? Stressed? Humorous? Amorous? (Hey, a guy can hope, right?). If you really want to SYNC UP with her, be sure to gauge her TONE so you can take it into account at this stage. Let's face it ... you won't get any points for goofing around when her TONE is serious or playing the heavy when she's feeling light-hearted.

TYPE is the category of communications. Did she ... ask a **Question**? ... Strike up a **Conversation**? ... Pay you a **Compliment**? ... Offer a **Critique**? ... Start to **Clash** with you? Knowing which TYPE of communications you're hearing offers clues about how best to SYNC UP.

Questions are inquiries, plain and simple.

Why is it that when the woman asks, "What are you wearing tonight?," the man hears, "Are you wearing *that*?" Instead, why not take the approach that when she asks a question, she wants to know more about you and your viewpoint — not judge you or give you the third degree. Welcome questions as her quick and easy ways to understand you better.

Conversation is a dialogue back and forth between the two of you.

As I stated earlier, enjoyable conversations can lead to

other enjoyable things. When you fuel her desire to connect, who knows what sparks might fly? You've got nothing to lose and plenty to gain. Consider getting in the mindset that conversations can bring you closer on a whole new level. Welcome conversations as opportunities for mutual exploration.

Compliments are flattering remarks shared between you.

Feel like she doesn't pay you enough compliments? Is it possible you don't notice when she does? Pay close attention – you may be getting more compliments than you think. Also, remember that compliments are a two-way street. Welcome the opportunity to give and get compliments — it doesn't cost you anything to "pay" someone a compliment.

Critiques are opinions or assessments offered between people when they feel close.

If you ever think, "Why does she always criticize me?" think again. According to her and the dictionary, critiques (opinions) are not the same as criticism (disapproval). Get in the frame of mind that when she offers you a critique, she feels close enough to open up and give you feedback so she can feel even closer to you. Sit back and enjoy the attention. Welcome the opportunity to get pointers from someone who really cares about you. You must value her opinions — she's your partner.

Clashes are contrasting viewpoints.

Let's not kid ourselves. Like all couples, the two of you are going to disagree from time to time. You can turn moments of dissonance into sweet harmony by focusing on what you agree on first before you get into the disagreement part. Remember that there is usually some common ground in any argument. Welcome the opportunity to focus on areas of overlap and, suddenly, your similarities can shine and your differences are put in their place – put into perspective.

Now for the payoff! On to Step 3.

Quick Tip

The Treasure Hunt

There's a lot to remember when you try to SYNC UP. You're processing what you see and hear, gearing up to respond vs. react. Think of it as a treasure hunt – LISTEN UP (Dig), SYNC UP (Discover), and SPEAK UP (say "Eureka! I found it!").

Step 3

Speak Up

Finally! Step 3. This is your chance to SPEAK UP and make a love connection.

Sound *Ridiculously Easy?*

- In Step 1, you intently LISTENED UP (maybe to the point of biting your lips off!) so her words didn't fall on deaf ears.

- In Step 2, you made sure to SYNC UP, taking the time to think about what she needs.

So it stands to reason that, right about now, you're experiencing some pent up demand to speak your mind. After all, relationships are a two-way street, aren't they?

While we know from Step 1 that she's not looking for the AnswerMan, she's not looking for a "Yes Man" either. While it's true that she definitely wants to hear from you right about now, as you might have guessed, there's a catch. Just as you're feeling the need to SPEAK UP, she's feeling pretty good about how well you've been listening! Believe me. If you're engaging in some effective listening, right about now she's thinking, "Did he just learn how to communicate with me?" Score! Clearly, you've earned some points — don't blow it now!

Now is the time to TELL her what you think in order to make a good love connection. So give her the old one-two punch. It will knock her socks off!

ONE-TWO PUNCH

ONE: REFLECT her viewpoint

Start by saying something to reflect or "mirror" back the essence of what you heard her say in Steps 1 and 2. For instance, if she tells you she "really had a hard day," try reflecting back with, "Pretty tough going, huh?" Of course, for a home run try also adding, "Do you want to talk about it?" If you remember back to Step 1, encouraging rapport-talk (vs. no talk) is a great way to earn some extra Brownie points. Now that you were able to LISTEN and SYNC, it should be easier for you to respond versus react. However, be sure to avoid repeating what she said word-for-word. Just like she doesn't want an AnswerMan or a Yes Man, she doesn't want an Ape Man either! If you mimic her verbatim, you run the risk of sounding insincere or condescending. And did I mention unoriginal?

TWO: SHARE your viewpoint

Now that you've proven to her you heard what she said by mirroring, you get to show her your stuff and add your own unique spin to the topic at hand. You've certainly earned it! Just remember that the more you LISTEN, SYNC, and REFLECT, the more likely you are to make a love connection.

When you SPEAK UP effectively, you have the power to change the game in your relationship. Like in a tennis match, instead of acing her out with a hard slam across the court you can suddenly enjoy a healthy volley back and forth across the net. Remember, the best score at the end of this match is LOVE — LOVE!

One thing to keep in mind is that sometimes, ironically, *Silence is Golden* when it comes to SPEAKING UP. For instance, if she's crying about something that's really upsetting to her, a warm hug and light kiss on the forehead can be more effective than saying a word.

Your own body language can speak volumes about how much you care.

Check out the following SPEAK UP *Dos and Don'ts* and you'll be an expert in no time.

SPEAK UP *DOS AND DON'TS*

Do you listen up?
If she says: "I can't resist all the goodies they sell at the farmers market!"

> **Don't say**: "Just leave your wallet in the car next time if you're so worried about it." (Sounds flip)

> **Do say**: "And I can't resist the dishes you create when you shop there!"

Do you reflect her tone?
If she says: "My day did not go well at all."

> **Don't say**: "Oh well. There's always tomorrow." (Sounds dismissive when she sounds sad)

> **Do say**: "Oh no, sorry to hear that. Tell me more!

Are you open to questions?
If she asks: "Did you put the dishes away yet?"

> **Don't say**: "No. I was too busy putting away the laundry." (Sounds defensive)

Do say: "I will, but first I'm finishing up the laundry."

Do you foster conversations?

If she says: "I really enjoyed that movie last night. What did you think?"

Don't say: "It was alright, I guess." (Closes off the opportunity to share)

Do say: "It was alright. The best part for me was seeing it with you! What did you like most about it?"

Do you enjoy a good compliment?

If she says: "I like those reading glasses much better on you. They make you look sexy!"

Don't say: "Thanks. What's for dinner?" (Ignores the compliment)

Do say: "Sexy, huh? I think I'll wear them more often."

Are you open to critique?

If she says: "That sweater is out of date … it's time to donate it."

Don't say: "It's fine — quit criticizing me!"

Do say: "But, I love this sweater. You gave it to me!"

Do you manage conflict?

If she says: "I completely disagree with you and, as usual, you are not listening to me at all."

> **Don't say:** "That's fine with me because you're all wrong anyway!"

> **Do say:** "OK, let's agree to disagree at least, OK?"

> **Or say:** "We disagree about most of it but we both really care about this so I am sure we can find common ground if we try."

Can you find common ground?

You can find common ground in any conflict…

> **Don't say:** "Are you kidding me? That makes no sense."

> **Do say:** "I see your point of view. I was thinking that too or how about this as an alternative."

Quick Tip

► The Extra Mile

As you prepare to SPEAK UP, look before you leap. If you're confused about something you heard or sensed, take a moment to ask a clarifying question. She'll appreciate you going the extra mile to understand her.

While this book is *Ridiculously Easy*, you can't expect perfection right out of the chute. There are going to be moments where you wish you had handled things differently. That's normal. Try the DVR Technique to help you rewind and reset as needed:

Rewind

If you would like to start over and respond differently to something you said or did, simply say, "Can I REWIND and try that again. I think I can do a better job of responding to you."

Reset

If an argument gets underway, simply say, "Can we RESET for a minute? Let's just reset our discussion starting with something we can both agree on."

Congratulations! You've arrived! You now have some powerful tools at hand to help you get along better with the special woman in your life! Hopefully some of the mystery is solved and you've gained some clarity into what makes her tick.

- You understand that she often values a trusted listening post versus the AnswerMan.

- You also understand that when you take the time to LISTEN UP and SYNC UP with her, you can respond instead of react, providing the rapport-talk she longs for.

Here's hoping the little toolset suggested in this book helps put you on better footing when it comes to happy, healthy communications! Remember, it's not as hard as you think to understand her. In fact, it's *Ridiculously Easy*!

Quick Tip

➤ Last-Minute Reminders

- **Do** be patient with yourself and your partner.
- **Do** have some fun with it.
- **Do** remember that practice makes perfect so practice, practice, practice!
- **Don't** expect things to change overnight.
- **Don't** expect too much – this is a communications tool, not a miracle cure.

TRACKING TOOLS

It's great that you've come this far and, to help you realize some gains, it's important to track your progress. Choose from the following three quick tracking tools, as needed:

- **Work Zone: Beginners.** This is a great place for everyone to start. It reminds you of the three basic steps — Listen Up/Sync Up/Speak Up — and their importance.

- **WorkZone: Advanced.** Once you know the three basic steps like the back of your hand, this tracker is a great way to brush up.

- **WorkZone: Interactive.** It takes two to tango with this tracker. You might want to get your sea legs with the other two trackers first and, by the time you get her involved in the tracking process, you'll be an ace. You never know … maybe you can make her a deal that if you get a good rating, she will "reward" you.

Good luck and remember: Practice makes perfect!

WORK ZONE: BEGINNERS

- Copy this page to use again and again.
- Write the topic of your communications.
- Circle your grade and make some notes.
- Repeat often to keep from getting rusty.

Topic	Listen Up	Sync Up	Speak Up
	☺	☺	☺
	☹	☹	☹
	☺	☺	☺
	☹	☹	☹
	☺	☺	☺
	☹	☹	☹
	☺	☺	☺
	☹	☹	☹
	☺	☺	☺
	☹	☹	☹

WORK ZONE: ADVANCED

- Copy this page to use again and again.
- Write the topic of your communications.
- Circle your grade.
- Keep notes on observations/ideas.
- Repeat often to keep from getting rusty.

Topic	Grade Yourself (circle one)	Notes
	😊 🙁	
	😊 🙁	
	😊 🙁	
	😊 🙁	
	😊 🙁	
	😊 🙁	
	😊 🙁	
	😊 🙁	
	😊 🙁	
	😊 🙁	
	😊 🙁	
	😊 🙁	
	😊 🙁	
	😊 🙁	
	😊 🙁	
	😊 🙁	

WORK ZONE: INTERACTIVE

- Copy this page to use again and again.
- Write the topic of your communications.
- Jot down the feedback your woman offers on your "performance."
- Jot down action items you plan to take.
- Repeat often to keep from getting rusty.

Topic	Rating (circle one)	Feedback	Action
	😊 😟		
	😊 😟		
	😊 😟		
	😊 😟		
	😊 😟		
	😊 😟		
	😊 😟		
	😊 😟		
	😊 😟		
	😊 😟		
	😊 😟		
	😊 😟		
	😊 😟		
	😊 😟		
	😊 😟		

REFERENCES

[1] Tannen, Ph.D., D. (1990). You just don't understand me: men and women in conversation. New York, NY: Harper Collins Publishers, New York, p. 77.

[2] Tannen, Ph.D., D. (1990). You just don't understand me: men and women in conversation. New York, NY: Harper Collins Publishers, p. 77.

[3] Gray, Ph.D., J. (1996). Mars and Venus Together Forever. New York. Harper Paperbacks.

Venus on fire mars on ice. Coquitlam, B.C.: Mind Publishing Inc., p. 2.

Gray takes the whole concept one step further in his 2010 book, *Venus on Fire Mars on Ice*, where he explains that the hormonal difference between men and woman goes a long way toward explaining "why men and women so often fail to 'get' one another." Under stress, women release oxytocin which helps them feel "safe, cooperative, caring, supportive and nurturing." Men, on the other hand, release testosterone, which works as "something of an emergency hormone" for "situations that require urgency, sacrifice for a noble cause and problem solving." This explains a lot about the communications gap discussed in this book. But, of course, it should not stop us from trying to bridge this hormonal gap or any gap in our day-to-day interactions with the one we love. www.mindpublishing.com p. 2

[4] Active Listening. In Wikipedia. Retrieved February 10, 2011, from http://en.wikipedia.org/wiki/Active_listening According to Wikipedia, the term "active listening" was coined by Thomas Gordon in his book "Leader Effectiveness Training." The article explains, "When interacting, people often are not listening attentively. They may be distracted, thinking about other things, or thinking about what they are going to say next ... . Active listening is a structured way of listening and responding to others, focusing attention on the speaker. Suspending one's own frame of reference, suspending judgment and avoiding other internal mental activities are important to fully attend to the speaker."

ABOUT THE AUTHOR

Paula Satow is a back-to-basics brand strategist, speaker and author. She has over 30 years of experience helping companies, groups and individuals discover their message, define their brand and build their marketing presence.

A serial entrepreneur, Paula founded brand marketing consultancy, Satow Strategies (www.SatowStrategies.com) and co-founded Buzzuka (www.Buzzuka.com), the website to create and promote powerful 30-second elevator pitches. She holds both bachelor's and master's degrees in media studies and communications. She is a dedicated "wabi-sabiist," and author of the upcoming book, *The Wabi-Sabi Way & Workbook*™.

Paula lives simply in Scottsdale, Arizona, with her husband, David, and their pet menagerie.

www.ingramcontent.com/pod-product-compliance
Lightning Source LLC
Chambersburg PA
CBHW071803020426
42331CB00008B/2394